OMNIBUS PRESS PRESENTS THE S...

RICKY MARTIN

Copyright © 1999 Omnibus Press
(A Division of Book Sales Limited)

Written by: Rene Cruz
Cover and Book Design by: Jade Romigin

US ISBN: 0-8256-1759-6
UK ISBN: 0-7119-7742-9

Exclusive distributors:
Book Sales Limited
8/9 Frith Street, London
W1V 5TZ, UK

Music Sales Corporation
257 Park Avenue South
New York City, NY 10010, USA

Music Sales PTY, Ltd
120 Rothschild Avenue
Roseberry, NSW 2018
Australia

To the Music Trade only:
Music Sales Limited,
8/9 Frith Street,
London W1V 5TZ, UK

Photo Credits:
Youri Lenquette/ Retna Ltd: Title Page, 11,
14, 19, 21, 26, 27, 31, 33, 34, 36, 42, 48
Sainlouis/ STILLS/Retna Ltd: 2, 17, 39
Scott Teitler/ Retna Ltd, USA: 5, 10, 20, 24/25,
Ernie Paniccioli/ Retna Ltd, USA: 6, 7 top, 7
bottom, 46/47
Robert Milazzo/ Retna Ltd, USA: 9
Neal Preston/ Retna Ltd: 13,
Steve Granitz/ Retna Ltd, USA: 15, 29, 44
Ron Wolfson/ LFI: 16, 35
Kelly Swift: 23
Kevin Mazur/ LFI: 30
R.Corlover: 37, 41
Joy E. Scheller/ LFI Int'l USA: 40
John Spellman/ Retna Ltd, USA: 45

Front Cover Photograph: Scott Teitler/
Retna Ltd, USA
Back Cover Photograph: Sainlouis/
STILLS/Retna Ltd

Printed in the United States of America by
Vicks Lithograph and Printing Corp.

It's about time! Ricky Martin, with his exuberant, sensual take on the world of pop music is just the slap in the face we all needed. And doesn't it hurt so good? Ever since his show-stopping performance at the 1999 Grammys, America has snapped to attention and leapt to its feet to revel in the throw-your-head-back abandon of music that's flaming hot and full of flavor.

All signs point to "Go" for Ricky Martin. The timing of his break into the U.S.A. couldn't be better. An industry and audience tired to the point of lethargic exhaustion with the current music scene is hungry, thirsty, and begging for a change. The menu of rap, alternative (alternately prepared with an angry, disillusioned, or just plain bored sauce), and over-choreographed, ultra-sweet teen outfits is in dire need of a special of the day. It seems that Puff Daddy and friends have over-recycled the hits of yesterday, and America is ready, willing, and able to embrace the sounds of salsa, merengue, samba, cumbia, bossa nova, batucada, and rock en español. *La vida loca* is looking, and sounding, damn good.

His first four solo albums have collectively racked up an impressive sales count of over thirteen million copies thus far, charting not only in his homeland, but as far afield as India, Europe, Israel, and Australia. A former member of teen act Menudo, he left his home and family in Puerto Rico when he was just twelve years old. He has acted on American television, starred on Broadway, and performed his 1998 World Cup theme song for an audience of two billion people. As sexy and charismatic as he is modest and fiercely private, this Latin superstar is poised to single-handedly start a musical revolution with his English-language debut album. So put your dancing shoes on, get those hips moving, and prepare yourself for a new wave of sounds that promise to put the hot-blooded passion back into pop music. To quote Ricky Martin's record-breaking single, "You'll never be the same . . ."

The sensation known today as Ricky Martin was born Enrique Martin Morales on December 24, 1971, in Puerto Rico's capital city, San Juan. His mother, Nereida Morales, an accountant, and father, Enrique Martin, a psychologist, split when he was only two years old, but to this day he remains extremely close with his half brothers and sister and indeed his entire extended family. Ricky has always remained intensely devoted to guarding his family, friends, and private life from the scrutiny that comes hand-in-hand with fame. As he told *USA Today* in its May 7, 1999, edition, "When I'm onstage, I have no secrets. But I try to protect the privacy of my room, my house, my friends, and my family."

It is music that Ricky loves to talk about, and it was music that captured his imagination as a child. Although today he is one of the foremost promoters of the joy of Latin sounds, as a boy he was more attracted to European and American pop—Journey, Boston, Cheap Trick, and David Bowie were early favorites. Ricky credits his mother with putting he and his siblings in touch with the music of their homeland, making Tito Puente and Celia Cruz concerts mandatory family excursions.

His flair for performing was evident from a very young age, when he delighted in acting in school plays, singing in choir, and was even overly zealous in his bell-ringing duties as an altar boy. At the ripe old age of six, Ricky announced to his papa that he wanted to be an artist. His father had an immediate reply for his little son; as Ricky oftentimes recalls, he asked, "How can I help?" Ricky made his professional debut in television commercials that very year. His artistic energies were channeled and honed in acting classes and singing lessons.

Young Ricky set his sights on the hottest sensation of the day, boy band Menudo, and was determined to become a member. Despite three failed auditions in which he was turned down due to his young age and short stature, in 1984 Ricky Martin (replacing Ricky Melendez) finally joined the group and set out on a five-year-long journey that would mold his future as an artist. Edgardo Díaz, Menudo's manager, told *Time* magazine in its May 24, 1999, issue, "He was small, not a big singer, and his voice was not so good then. But we thought he could learn a lot by being with the group."

It is quite amazing that at the age of twelve, a mild-mannered young boy from a close-knit family could simply up and leave home to pursue such a demanding career, but this was what Ricky was meant to do. As he told MTV's Serena Altschul in May 1999, "Everything was so fast—I was only twelve. I just wanted to be up there and sing and dance." Photos of the angelic, tiny little Ricky in his requisite parachute pants and sequined tank top show just how young he really was at the outset. But he had no doubts or regrets; he knew he was following his dreams. His parents had realistically and responsibly prepared their son for the difficulties and demands of a show business life, although they themselves hadn't experienced such a thing first-hand. Ricky was able, somehow, to keep himself grounded during the adrenaline-powered rush of fame, applause, and adoration. Of course, at the onset of his time spent in the spotlight, Ricky was the baby of the group. "When I was fourteen, I started to get the chills around older women, but they would always say, 'Ohh, cute little Ricky!'" he confessed to *People* magazine in its 1999 "Fifty Most Beautiful" issue. Looking back to his formative teenage years spent in the fish-bowl of success, Ricky claims to have reminded himself each and every day that it would end at some point, and made the mature decision to learn as much as he could

from the experience for future use rather than getting caught up in the moment. "To anyone who is in a boy band now, I wish you the best of luck," he advised on *MTV News 1515* in May 1999. "Enjoy it, learn from it, be a sponge—it's not gonna last forever."

Of the Menudo experience, which didn't last forever for any of its members due to its strict age-limit booting policy, Ricky told Gloria Estefan during his June 1999 *Interview* magazine feature, "It was five years of discipline, Gloria. It was military. . . . In Menudo I'd see 250,000 people from the stage in Brazil, and days later there would be fifteen people watching us, and the manager would say, 'You're going to perform like it's 250,000 people.' You learn to appreciate. That's why each interview I do, each television program I appear on, it's going to be like it's the first one or the last one." Discipline was definitely the name of the game, and the youngsters spent as much time on planes as on stage, performing in English, Spanish, or Portuguese, depending on which country the show was in on a given night. Stories of troubles in the Menudo camp spread like wildfire, and it was rumored that many of its members came out of the group with problems, but as Díaz recalled to *Time* magazine in its May 24, 1999, issue, "Ricky had that special personality, like a charm. He could handle himself." Robi Rosa, ex-Menudo member and present-day Ricky Martin musical collaborator and producer, explained the teen stardom situation to *Time* magazine in its May 10, 1999, issue, stating, "Two things can happen when you join a group like Menudo. You can get all messed up, or you can pay attention and learn from it. We learned a lot. For Ricky and me, the studio is like home now."

Having reached the set "outing" age, and ready to move on, in 1989 Ricky left Menudo and returned home to finish high school. He then set out for New York to lead a normal life for a short while, hanging out in Manhattan and soaking up all the facets of the thriving city. Ricky felt that the Big Apple was the perfect place to "do nothing," as there was so much happening around him—he could take time to simply observe and reflect. He consciously decided not to dive headlong into a solo career immediately following his departure from an ultra-successful act. Wisely, he took this time to redefine his own personality outside of the group. As he told Serena Altschul in his MTV interview, "I needed to stop and just detach from anything that had to do with show business, because I was, first of all, saturated. Second of all, I didn't know who I was. I didn't know what I liked. I didn't know what I hated. Why? Because [I was] part of a concept."

He has also professed to being relieved to move on from Menudo because he is, in his own words, a control freak. "I left the band because I wanted to have all the control and all the responsibilities," he told Katie Couric in his March 12, 1999, *Today Show* interview. "And it feels good!" His period of introspection complete, Ricky moved to Mexico to pursue both acting and singing. He played a character named Pablo in the popular Mexican soap opera *Alcanzar Una Estrella*; Pablo was a musician in a pop group called Muñecos de Papel. The daytime television show was so popular that the band actually went on tour in Mexico, and the storyline of the drama was transformed into a film. Ricky's performance in the movie version of *Alcanzar Una Estrella* won him a Heraldo Award (Mexico's Academy Award).

In the midst of all of this success, Sony signed the popular performer to Sony Discos, the company's Latin imprint, and released his debut solo album, *Ricky Martin*, in 1991. The album was an instant success, garnering gold records in Puerto Rico, Chile, Mexico, and Argentina, and securing Ricky's star status in Latin America. Opening with a string-laden ballad "Fuego Contra Fuego," the album offered bass, horn, and beat-driven light dance tunes like "Dime Que Me Quieres" ("Bring a Little Lovin") and a spattering of emotive slow tunes; it was basically a compilation of Spanish-language pop songs. Stand-out touches like the young voice choir on "Te Voy a Conquistar (Vou te Conquistar)," the rock guitar solos on "Corazon Entre Nubes (Coracao Nas Nuvens)," and the live audience participation on "Susana" added texture to the album, and Ricky's voice is nicely showcased throughout. Equally showcased were the now grown-up singer's good looks—the album cover features a tanned Ricky, long curls blowing in the breeze, in an open-chested waistcoat; the back cover artwork offers the artist lying in the ocean, his white tank top and jeans soaking wet.

Ricky followed up with May 1993's *Me Amaras*, arranged by Juan Carlos Calderon, whose long list of credits include work with artists from Boyz II Men and Luis Miguel to Placido Domingo. This sophomore effort also rocketed to the top of the Latin charts, backing up the album's title, which translates to "You Will Love Me." The May 8, 1993, *Billboard* review of the album described Ricky as a "young Puerto Rican balladeer who benefits greatly on this soothing pop album from Calderon's hyper-romantic yarns and crisp production." The album was indeed a smoother, slower-paced album than its predecessor, featuring many pleasing tracks with more of an adult-contemporary flair than the straightforward pop of his debut. The production was certainly superior, if a little overdone overall. Fans ate it up, but critics couldn't help but point out its weaknesses.

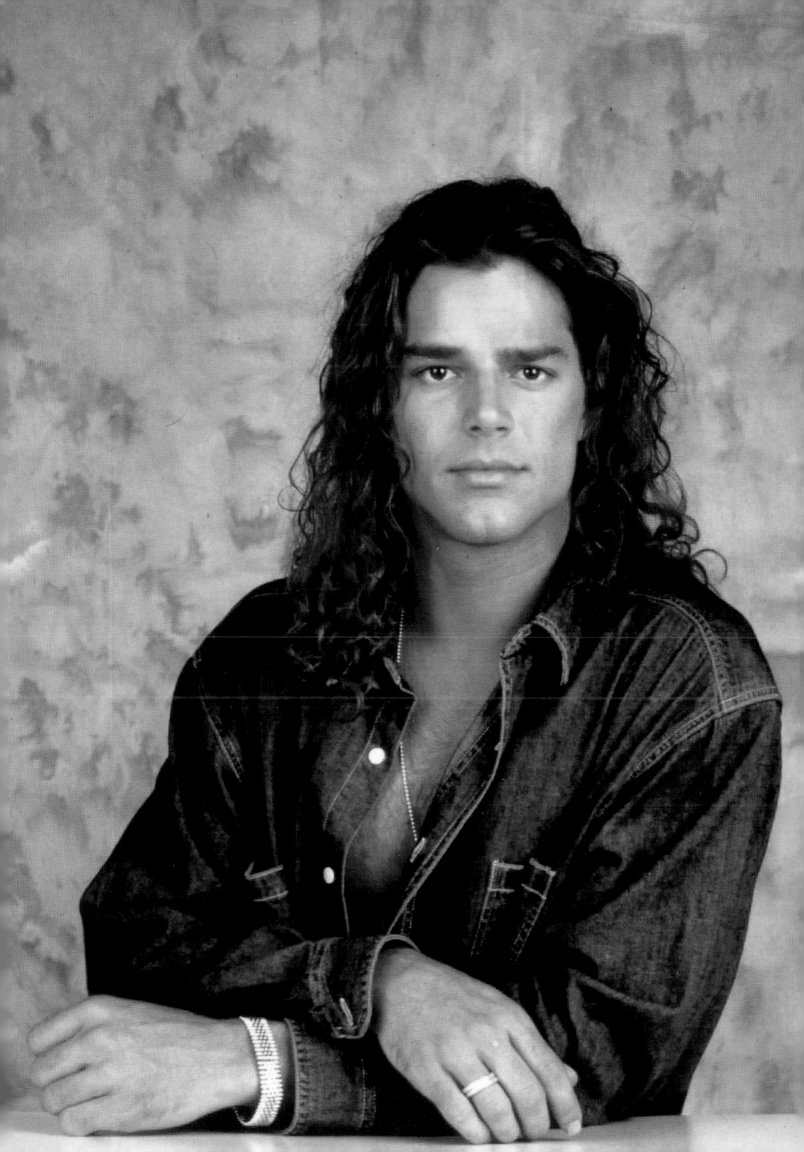

Alex Henderson's *All-Music Guide* review labeled the album "too glossy, too calculated and much too contrived for its own good," complaining that, "Few chances are taken on this by-the-book release, which seldom fails to sound like a product of the corporate music machine."

An unusual feature of *Me Amaras* is the Spanish cover version of Laura Branigan's 1984 hit "Self Control," "Que Dia Es Hoy." The title track steps up the beat a little, and spices things up with horns, but Ricky still had not realized his musical potential. The closing number, "Hooray! Hooray! (It's a Holi-Holiday)" rather unfortunately brings to mind cruise-ship sing-alongs. This album's artwork presents a more sophisticated image—Ricky's still-long locks are more groomed, and his sunglassed, suited look is more New Romantic than old Menudo.

With two albums under his belt, Ricky Martin was well on his way, and sold-out concerts all over South America followed. An exciting milestone was his winning "Best New Latin Artist" at the 1993 Billboard Music Awards.

Ricky moved to Los Angeles at the end of the year to pursue his acting, and after spots of television work joined the cast of long-running U.S. soap opera *General Hospital* in February 1994, as bartender/musician Miguel Morez. The show's executive producer Wendy Riche was sold after just one meeting with the aspiring actor, and allegedly decided on the spot to invent a character for the charismatic young man. As she would years later tell *Time* magazine in its May 10, 1999, issue, "He lives to perform." "People just love and adore Ricky," actress Lilly Melgar, who played Ricky's character's girlfriend on the show, was to tell *People* magazine in its 1999 "Fifty Most Beautiful" issue. "He has a regal presence with the spirit of a child."

Ricky, as Miguel, experienced his share of daytime-drama-style twists and turns during his stint with the show. His character landed a record deal, and was shipped back to his native land of Puerto Rico for a career-launching concert where he found his long-lost love, Lily Rivera, the daughter of the country's top crime boss. Dramatic enough? Not quite—the newly reunited couple then located their six-year-old son who Lily's disapproving mobster father had forced her to give up for adoption. But alas, it all ended in heartache for Miguel. Ricky himself, in much better spirits than his character, left the show after some two years to move on to the next challenge in his career: a role in Broadway sensation *Les Miserables.*

You might think that all of this was keeping our Ricky a little busy, but let's not forget whom we are dealing with. In the midst of his blossoming acting career, Ricky was not ignoring his musical ambitions, and made the time to release his third solo album in October 1995, entitled *A Medio Vivir* ("To Half Live" or "To Live Halfway"). It was with this album that Ricky hooked up with his true musical partners, fellow ex-Menudo member Robby Rosa, now known as Robi Rosa (on this album working under the pseudonym Ian Blake), and K.C. Porter. Ricky is consistently lavish when it comes to singing the praises of Robi. "I think he's a genius. From the age of twelve he was always in front of the piano," he told Latin Music On-Line in Little Judy's March 31, 1996, interview. "I talk about him everywhere, everywhere. When people ask me, I tell them that I'm very proud to be working with him. He has so much to give." K.C. Porter is known for work with the likes of Patti LaBelle, Los Fabulosos Cadillacs, New Edition, Selena, Toni Braxton, and even sang background vocals on Robi Rosa's own 1994 solo album *Frio.* He has also been instrumental in aiding the likes of Boyz II Men and Janet Jackson to truly cross over to the Latin market by translating their songs into Spanish. Porter and "Blake" shared producing, arranging, writing, programming, and engineering credits on *A Medio Vivir.* Benny Faccone (who was thanked by Ricky on *Me Amaras*—"During times of desperation you always asked me for one more take, 'for you.' Somehow you knew that one would be the best one.") was once again part of the team as engineer and mixer. The album artwork is the work of a photographer who was soon to make his name as one of the prominent rock photographers in the business: David LaChapelle, and the shots of a casual, sun-streaked Ricky are much more genuine than the posed, calculated visuals of his previous albums.

A Medio Vivir was truly a breakthrough for Ricky, treating fans new and old to the kick-off of his soon-to-be signature combination of musical styles and Latin sounds. From hard rock to flamenco, from cumbia to a touch of techno, the album manages to pull together many genres to form a cohesive whole. The songs, benefiting from the

songwriting skills of Porter, Blake/Rosa, Luis Gómez Escolar, and others—including, on the heartfelt ballad "Volveras," Ricky himself—are far superior to those found on his first two releases. The guitar-driven "Revolucion" became a live concert highlight, complete with a military stage treatment. A standout track is the original version of "Maria," a flamenco-flavored hit that was to be transformed into an even bigger hit in the future.

The October 7, 1995, *Billboard* review claimed, "*General Hospital* heartthrob from Puerto Rico comes up with his strongest effort yet, thanks to producers K.C. Porter and Ian Blake." "Everything that you listen to in this album, that's my life," Ricky told Little Judy in a March 31, 1996, Latin Music On-Line interview. "I sat with different composers and told them what I wanted to express; what I was going through at that moment of my life and how I wanted to approach the audience with that album." Ricky thanks Robi, K.C., and Benny on the album liner notes, for those "who capture my feelings, recorded them and made them sound incredible for their wit and wisdom. But also for those times of happiness and laughter in moments of desperation." *A Medio Vivir* was certified Gold in the United States in October 1997.

Ricky took advantage of his *General Hospital*-free schedule in the spring of 1996 to put his dancing shoes back on. Ricky's March 30, 1996, sold-out show at New York's Radio City Music Hall was a small premonition of the fan-demonium that was to greet him in the States in years to come. A few crazed female fans even managed to foil security and leap onstage to attack the singer with hugs and kisses. Sandwiched in between this high-profile gig and his Broadway debut, Ricky took a bit of time to himself once again.

"I'm always surrounded by people," he explained to Little Judy in his March 31, 1996, Latin Music On-Line interview. "I mean it's great because they're friends; they're people that I work with and people that I enjoy spending time with. But I need more time to be alone, just to put my thoughts in order. Just to realize what I'm doing and what I want to do." Years later, in a 1999 interview with MTV VJ Serena Altschul, Ricky elaborated on his method of dealing with moments of fear and weakness, times when the sacrifices of success seem overwhelming and the desire to lock himself in his house is very tempting. He explained, "So for me [it's] so important to take my time and just talk to myself and analyze what I've done. Step out of the picture, look at the picture, look what you've done, look where you are, look where you want to get, and then go back to the picture with a healthier way of thinking."

So, back to the lights and sawdust: Ricky hit the stage in a big way when he landed a limited engagement with *Les Miserables*. How did he manage to get the part? It is rumored that during an interview he gave while still acting on *General Hospital*, Ricky was asked what his goals were before leaving this earth, and his reply was that he had always wanted to do theater on Broadway. Allegedly the producer of *Les Mis* read the interview and called him in for an audition! His three-month run with the show began in June 1996 at New York City's Imperial Theater. Ricky took on the role of student revolutionary Marius after meeting with the show's executive producer Richard Jay-Alexander, who was confident that Ricky's vocal and acting skills, along with his onstage charisma, would suit the part. Ricky's role in the Broadway staple set in 19th century Paris showcased his moving singing voice through the duet "A Heart Full of Love" and the ballad "Empty Chairs at Empty Tables." "Theater was great. That's my favorite," Ricky would years later rave to MTV's Serena Altschul. "That's exactly when you have to really understand the meaning of the word 'discipline.' It's seven shows a week, and it's three hours on stage. . . . You're dealing with a different audience in front of you every night. If you want a standing ovation, you have to sweat. So it's draining. I have a lot of respect for theater actors, especially those that have been doing a part for ten years. If you can do that, you can do anything you want in life. And I loved it."

Ricky was still performing a balancing act between his love of acting and theater and his passion for music. In the spring of 1997 it was officially announced that he had extended his worldwide recording agreement with Sony Music International.

In the summer of 1997 Disney's new animated film *Hercules* hit the cinemas. What does another box-office smash kiddy flick have to do with Ricky Martin? Well, in the Spanish version of the film, which was shown in selected markets in the United States and throughout Latin America, the voice of Hercules himself was provided by none other than our Ricky. He also sang the Spanish and Portuguese version of the film's end-credit song, "No Importa la Distancia" (the English version, "Go the Distance," was recorded by Michael Bolton).

That same summer the dance version of "(Un Dos Tres) Maria" was a huge hit in France and all over Europe, where Ricky was labeled the "Latin George Michael." Mix master Pablo Flores had remixed the *A Medio Vivir* album version of "Maria," giving the formerly flamenco-influenced song a samba-driven, faster beat. The resulting track was a best-selling 1997 single in Europe, and gained considerable airplay and popularity in the United States. In Japan, the song was used in a television ad Ricky participated in for Suzuki. On November 20, 1997, Ricky won an award for "The Latino Artist with the Greatest International Impact" at Spain's Premios Amigo Awards held in Madrid. Ricky Martin was fast on his way to becoming a household name in countries all around the globe.

It was through one of the world's biggest sporting events that Ricky Martin's name was truly branded into the general public's collective mind. His song "La Copa de la Vida," penned by the super-team of Robi Rosa, Desmond Child, and Luis Gómez Escolar, was the official theme song of the 1998 World Cup soccer tournament. In December 1997 it was announced that the samba song with the irresistible Brazilian batucada beats would be the international theme song for the event. Youssou N'Dour and Axelle Red's "La Cour Des Grands" was to be the official French anthem, and both songs were performed at the December 4 draw ceremony in Marseilles, France. "The song could literally take me around the world," Ricky told *Billboard* in its February 14, 1998, issue. "It is a little intimidating, but we are going out there with knives in our mouths and [will] work this record and fight for what we can get." Looks like a little fighting spirit can go a long way. "La Copa de la Vida" went on to become a roaring success, hitting Number One on Music & Media's Eurochart Hot 100 Singles chart and selling millions worldwide.

Naturally, "La Copa de la Vida" ("The Cup of Life") was the first single issued from Ricky's fourth solo album, *Vuelve*. Ricky celebrated *Vuelve's* release with two shows in Puerto Rico. The 50,000 or so fans at each of the February 12 and 13, 1998, concerts at San Juan's Hiram Bithorn Stadium, were happy to join him in partying in the album's honor, which debuted at Number One on *Billboard's* Latin charts. *Vuelve* was destined to be a world-wide success. Not only had Ricky's musical style, prowess, and confidence grown and grown over the last three albums, but Sony was behind him all the way on this one. Promotional campaigns were launched in many countries, from Japan to Europe to Southeast Asia, where a pre-release promo CD was issued by Sony Music Asia containing three "Spanglish" versions of "Maria" along with an English version of "The Cup of Life."

On *Vuelve*, the arranging, producing, and writing team of K.C. Porter and Robi Rosa included a third member in Desmond Child, rock writer and producer extraordinaire perhaps best known for his work with Aerosmith, Jon Bon Jovi, Alice Cooper, Michael Bolton, Kiss, and newest British invasion sensation Robbie Williams. Child was immediately convinced of Ricky's certain U.S. success. As he later told *Entertainment Weekly* in its April 23, 1999, issue, "Latin stars have been trying to cross over for a long time. A lot of it just sits there. Ricky's a prince who's been groomed to be king." The album was recorded in studios in California, Miami, Madrid, and Puerto Rico. It is *Vuelve's* artwork that presents the Ricky Martin America was soon to fall head-over-heals in love with: sophisticated, sexy, self-possessed, and showing off his irresistible smile.

The album opens with a celebratory fanfare of a song in "Por Arriba, Por Abajo," which proves a bang-on-target guarantee of the exceptional selection of music to follow. The title track "Vuelve" ("Come Back") showcases a new level of ballads for Ricky; it is multitextured and plays upon the strengths of his voice with wonderful effect. "Gracias por Pensar En Mi" ("Thank You for Thinking of Me") is a song written by Renato Russo, who died of AIDS just after writing the song. Elements of salsa can be found in "Lola, Lola." The addictive samba-style rhythm of "La Bomba" would find itself hitting the airwaves as yet another strong single. A layered wealth of tropical, sensual, exciting rhythms, *Vuelve* definitely gets the heart pumping and the blood flowing.

Billboard's February 28, 1998, review called the *Vuelve* "a package of meaty, bittersweet romantic ballads and chest-pumping, upbeat numbers." The Dallas *Morning News's*

review of the album chose to focus on the slow tracks "that keep teenage girls coming back for more. The title cut, a sultry love song with a sexy refrain, makes the best of his powder-keg vocals" and labeled "Perdido Sin Ti" "a bedroom staple." The beauty of Ricky's fourth solo effort is that it is strong and skillful on both sides of the coin. All in all, the album is suffused with confidence, energy, and an undeniable love of the music.

First *Hercules,* then *Zorro!* The summer of 1998 saw another hit film featuring the singing voice of Ricky Martin as he teamed up with Australia's hot female artist Tina Arena to sing the movie's theme song "I Want to Spend the Rest of My Life Loving You" written by James Horner and Will Jennings, musical masterminds behind the Titanic mega-hit "My Heart Will Go On."

Through well-received singles and the hard, hard work Ricky put in throughout 1997 touring and promoting in Europe, as well as his springtime European promotional run, Ricky Martin was officially a success with a capital "S" in that part of the world. It all culminated in Ricky's performance of "La Copa de la Vida" at the Summer 1998 World Cup Final in front of two billion TV viewers—alleged to be the world's largest television audience ever—which was nothing short of triumphant.

Alas, you can't avoid politics, not even if you're a hot young recording artist with the world at your feet. It seems that the lyrics of "La Copa de la Vida"—in particular the verse, *"You have to fight for a star"*—along with the crowd-rallying beat of the music proved itself irresistible to Puerto Rico's New Progressive Party, whose goal is to have Puerto Rico deemed the U.S.A.'s fifty-first state. Govenor Pedro Rossell adopted the World Cup single as his party's own theme song at a July 25, 1998, rally in Guanica, Puerto Rico, where he gave a speech calling for the star of his country's flag to be stitched "onto the flag of the great American nation, where it rightfully belongs." The political party conceded that their use of the song was not authorized by Ricky Martin, and Ricky's manager Angelo Medina insisted that the artist is apolitical, telling *Billboard* in its September 5, 1998, issue, "Music doesn't choose sides. It belongs to everyone," adding, "Ricky is the finest product Puerto Rico has to promote itself internationally." Desmond Child, a co-writer of the song, told Billboard that "La Copa" "is strictly about world unity and the World Cup. We weren't rooting for anybody. It was meant to be about the games and sportsmanship." Which indeed it was. Regardless of a little controversy, "La Copa de la Vida" was one of the most memorable songs of the year.

Rest on his laurels? Of course not. *Allez! Allez! Allez!* Ricky set out to conquer Asia with a concert tour in Japan and Southeast Asia supported by a television campaign. The Japanese and Asian music markets took a shine to Ricky due to the World Cup connection as well as the success of "Maria." Emi Hatano of Epic in Japan explained Sony's willingness to promote the Latin singer to *Billboard* in its February 14, 1998, issue, "because he is good-looking and after receiving all of the news elsewhere that he is doing great, we became very interested in him." Sony Music Asia's Yvonne Yuen's reasoning was, "Soccer is huge in Asia, and 'The Cup of Life' will offer the perfect opportunity to take advantage of it. . . . So what we want to do is to introduce consumers to a great singer who has the whole package." Asia embraced Ricky Martin and his music; he was an enormous success in India. How to explain this unexpected popularity in such disparate cultures? As Ricky insisted to *USA Today* in its May 7, 1999, edition, "It doesn't matter where you're from. If you have a soul, you're going to be attached to [Latin] rhythms." Ricky credits the primal pounding beat of the drums as the driving force behind the universal appeal of music. "It doesn't matter if you're from Sweden, from South Africa, from Australia, or from the Caribbean, it's going to be part of your body. You're going to dance," he insisted in the June 1999 issue of *Interview* magazine. "When we are in the womb, we feel the beat of our mother's heart. That's how it started."

Although Ricky hadn't officially "broken" in the United States as yet, over 10,000 fans attended his sold-out concert at Anaheim, California's Arrowhead Pond on October 24, 1998. The show placed Ricky Martin in the top ten of *Amusement Business*'s Boxscore listings, in the company of two Mexican acts, Mana and Juan Gabriel. A week later Ricky celebrated Halloween by singing and dancing the night away in front of some 14,000 fans at New York City's Madison Square Garden on October 31. Members of the audience may have been dressed up as ghosts and ghouls in honor of the holiday, but Ricky hit the stage in his usual impeccable garb, opening in a beautifully cut charcoal gray suit, and treating the crowd to a revolving ensemble of outfits. His band and back-up singers were also well dressed, and with the dry ice and smoke, the atmosphere could well have been a runway show were it not for the pounding Latin beat and musical spontaneity. Mainstream U.S. music audiences may never have heard of Ricky Martin, but for an unknown he certainly had a huge following. And, as the months to come would prove, Americans hadn't seen nothin' yet.

December 1998 found Ricky performing to an all-new audience in Singapore; his show for a crowd of some 4,500 at the Harbour Pavilion was a rousing success. In true breakthrough style, Ricky went on to make history as the first Hispanic artist to perform in China, where his concert in Beijing's Gongren Stadium defied cultural and language boundaries. Spain again welcomed their favorite Latin star at the end of the year when he recorded a Television Española Christmas special.

Ricky Martin is an experienced performer, and knows what works on stage. His acting skills are very useful in adding a new dimension to his show. Role-playing is most definitely a part of his performance; aside from multiple costume changes, he takes on different personas throughout his shows to further emphasize the mood of each song. For the sensual "Vuelve," he is as suave as they come, with the effortless footwork and hypnotic moves of a seducer. A throw-reason-to-the-wind abandon seems to overtake him when he takes on the driving Latin rhythms of his faster songs, and the excitement

and power-hungry attitude of an avid sports fan is evident whenever he performs "La Copa de la Vida." Early in his career, he took to occasionally performing certain songs *a cappella*, such as his debut album's "El Amor de Mi Vida," to contrast the beat-driven nature of most of his show. A touching speech about AIDS awareness precedes his performance of "Gracias Por Pensar en Mi," while a thirty-strong choir adds beauty and drama to "Vuelve" and additional percussionists pack an extra wallop to "Maria." Ricky is in his element when he is onstage, and treats each and every performance as if it were his one and only. "The feeling that I get when I'm on stage . . . I will never change that for anything. It gives you strength, it gives you some kind of power, it gives you control. What do I want to be doing in thirty years? I want to do this; I want to do music. Let's keep studying, let's keep getting ready." Ricky told Gloria Estefan during his June 1999 *Interview* magazine feature, "When you're up there in concert and you come down from that adrenaline, you have to be careful because it can be 'boom'-and it can be really painful when you hit the floor." Oftentimes at the close of his shows, he tells the audience, "I leave my heart and soul on this stage tonight. I hope you do the same, too."

Ricky Martin celebrated the New Year by wrapping up the recording of his English-language debut, an album that had been two years in the making. At least, he thought he had finished work on what he hoped would be the instrument strong enough to break him in America, but one little evening was destined to take care of that for him, as well as put just one more track on the album's song list . . . look out, it's Grammy time!

The Rosie O'Donnell-hosted 1999 Grammy Awards ceremony on February 24 may have been dominated by the fairer sex—winners Celine Dion, the Dixie Chicks, Shania Twain, Alanis Morissette, Brandy, Monica, Sheryl Crow, and Madonna shared the podium with Lauryn Hill who walked away with five golden statues—but it was one mere man who stole the show.

In front of well over one billion viewers in close to 200 countries, Ricky Martin delivered a show-stopping performance of "La Copa de la Vida." Clad in leather trousers, he rhumba'd, samba'd, salsa'd, swiveled, and twisted his way into everyone's hearts within moments. He had quite a cast of back-up singers, dancers, and a hell of a group of musicians backing him up, but even without the big production it is certain he could have pulled it off. It was his immediately infectious enthusiasm and love of the music, the performance, and the night itself, that brought the jaded, show-biz crowd to its feet. Here was an artist who was truly thrilled to be there, and his excitement-filled attitude galvanized the usual tired old award show and took it to a completely higher level. To get a standing ovation from an audience made up of the top musical artists of the day is truly a feat.

Ricky is deservedly delighted with the memory of his Grammy coup. Of course, it's a piece of cake to get up on stage in front of hordes of adoring fans, but this was different: Ricky was strutting his stuff to the very artists he most admired—the cream of the crop, everyone who had Made It. As he told *MTV News 1515*, "I'm performing in front of the industry. I mean, these people, they've heard it all, they've seen it all—what am I gonna do?" The answer? "Go out there and have fun." He repeatedly recalls being "anxious," but, as he told *Entertainment Weekly* in its April 23, 1999, issue, "I said, 'Dude, you've been doing this for fifteen years. Just be yourself.' Then I went, 'Hey, Sting, you know what? Check this out, bro.' I knew he'd remember me." And Sting isn't the only one. Ricky mischievously recalled the superstar-studded crowd dancing, clapping, and generally getting down with his performance when he told *Time* magazine in its May 15, 1999, issue, "To see Will Smith doing the jiggy with my song! It's overwhelming."

Even Madonna, ever in front of the latest trend, was swept away by the infectious energy and enthusiasm of Ricky's wake-up-call performance, and reportedly made a backstage beeline for the Latin up-and-comer. Martin downplays the Grammy meeting with the reigning queen of pop. "We had met before," he told the Los Angeles *Times* in its April 19, 1999, edition. "We actually worked together as part of the cast for a TV show in Austria. And we've met a couple of times here in Miami. But ever since [the Grammy awards] she's been very excited about working with me." Of course, any sort of connection between Madonna and a hot young man—particularly a hot young man destined to be the next big thing—sparks a bit of light-hearted gossip-mongering. The *Village Voice's* Scott Seward couldn't resist naming Ricky "Least Likely to Escape without Madonna Raping Him" in his March 9, 1999, report on the Grammys.

Attempting to explain what happened that fated February 24 night at Los Angeles'

Shrine Auditorium, Ricky told Katie Couric during his March 12, 1999, *Today Show* appearance, "What I presented that evening . . . was special because of the cultural exchange I tried to create. I guess people are willing to feel new things with new rhythms and the Latin sounds that I was performing that night." The truth of the matter was, Ricky Martin is a tremendous performer, and his genuine enjoyment was a breath of fresh and fabulous air to everyone that evening. It was no stretch of the imagination to envision millions of TV viewers jumping up off of their couches to catch the kiss he threw to the audience. To his "La Copa de la Vida" cry of "Do you really want it?" the answer was a resounding "Yeah!"

Ricky's Grammy for Best Latin Pop Performance for Vuelve was applauded by more than a few industry insiders. As Los Angeles *Times'* Ernesto Lechner wrote in the paper's February 25, 1999, issue, "By giving a Latin pop performance Grammy to Ricky Martin over more conservative crooners, the voters sent a symbolic message to the industry: It is still possible to craft an album that captures the magic of decades past while sounding hip and contemporary." Following in the footsteps of Celia Cruz and Gloria Estefan, Ricky was the third artist to sing in Spanish at the Grammys. When it was announced in January that Ricky Martin would perform a bilingual rendition of his World Cup hit at the ceremony, Michael Greene, President/CEO of the Recording Academy commented, "We are delighted to have such a talented performer on the 41st Annual Grammy Awards. As both an actor and performer, he brings a special energy to the show. We are also committed to represent more Latin Music in our future endeavors."

And how did the crowd back home enjoy the festivities? Ricky's family and friends threw a Grammy party, Latin-style, and were reportedly delighted with their man's successful evening. As he grinningly told Rosie O'Donnell, his mother "was crying. . . . She was in Puerto Rico but she was the first person I spoke to." Surely with the whole world watching, Ricky must have felt a little stress before the show. He has admitted to preparing backstage with his trusty Kriya Yoga. As he humorously revealed to *Rolling Stone* in its April 29, 1999, issue, "I thought I'd have to stick my toe in my ear, but it's all about connecting your heart and your mind to get to a point where you get to hear the beat of your heart and the sound of the blood running through your veins. It's really intense." Intensely effective, if his performance that night owed itself in any way to the practice.

Sales of *Vuelve* directly following the show-stopping telecast went right through the roof. Gringos who had never ventured into the Latin section of their local record stores were storming the shelves looking for Ricky Martin CDs. The album was in such incredible demand after the Grammys that the very day after the show aired Ricky's label quite literally ran out of copies, and had to effect an emergency print run to fill the feverish rash of orders coming in from chains all over the country. "We were caught completely off-guard," Sony Discos vice president of sales Jeff Young admitted to *Billboard* in its May 13, 1999, issue. Who wasn't?

Ricky had the American music industry and public on the edge of their seats, and he brought them right back on their feet again, hitting them with his best shot, a riotously irresistible romp of pulsating Latin rhythms, sucker-punching horns, and ska/rock/you name it beats called "Livin' La Vida Loca." Livin' the crazy life, it seemed, was just what we were hoping Ricky Martin would propose. The fabulous video gave an audience teased by his Grammy whammy a full dose of hip-swinging, eye-twinkling Ricky, with a night-on-the-town theme complete with short-skirted dancers, checkerboard dance floors, and a stunning Croatian model for a female protagonist.

At the end of April the single rocketed to the top of Soundscan's single chart, selling some 280,000 copies in its first week of release, and making history as the first time a Latin male had hit the top spot (not to mention that it had been over a year since a male of any description had reached Number One). *Billboard* deemed, "If there was ever a song that you knew was a hit the first time you heard it, this is it," in its April 17, 1999, issue. "This really gives the public a brand-new sound," Tommy Mottola said to *USA Today* in its May 7, 1999, edition. "The rhythms are such a fusion of R&B, pop, jazz, and Latin music. . . . It becomes a pop record that people can relate to, but it's something completely different." The song was officially one of the best-selling Number One singles in U.S. history, joining the illustrious ranks of the likes of Elton John and übersongstress Celine Dion. That very same month, *Vuelve* was certified Platinum. The "Livin' La Vida Loca: The Remixes" CD Single included the "Track Masters Remix," featuring rappers Big Pun (a.k.a. Big Punisher) and Fat Joe; the Track Masters production credits also include Nas and Foxy Brown. In May 1999 Ricky made more history by becoming the first artist to simultaneously hold the Number One slot on the Billboard Hot 100, Top 40 Tracks, Hot Latin Tracks, and Hot Dance Music/Maxi-Singles Sales charts. Ladies and gentleman, Ricky Martin has entered the building.

February through March saw Ricky on an extensive promotion campaign in Mexico, Los Angeles, Europe, Miami, back to L.A., and again to Mexico, then on to Argentina. Upon the release of "Livin' La Vida Loca" he hit the U.S.A., Canada, and his homeland Puerto Rico for further promotional efforts. Despite the fact that every respectable pop music-lover in the land was strutting down the street to a new, Latin beat, Ricky wasn't about to let up on his onslaught on America's senses.

Ricky was everywhere. He joined the cast of performers at the last minute at the Ninth Annual Rainforest Foundation Benefit concert, along with seasoned superstars Sting (co-founder of the event with his wife Trudie Styler), James Taylor, Elton John, Billy Joel, Tony Bennett, Don Henley, and Charles Aznavour. Ricky made the most of his rendition of "I've Got the World on a String" during the concert, a tribute to the late Frank Sinatra held in New York City's Carnegie Hall on April 17. The Los Angeles *Times*, in its April 19, 1999 edition, reported that "Latin heartthrob Ricky Martin, who swiveled his hips and struck cocky Sinatra poses in a gray suit and porkpie hat, exuded an unstoppable mix of self-confidence and exuberance." The word on the street was that, once again, he blew them all away. The beauty of it is, he does it with a smile, and even the hardest, meanest, most competitive and egotistical rock star around can't help but love it.

Following the Grammys, Luciano Pavarotti himself allegedly picked up the phone to invite the young hot shot to be one of the performers at 1999's "Pavarotti and Friends"

annual benefit for the Warchild organization, along with Mariah Carey, Gloria Estefan, B.B. King, Joe Cocker, Boyzone, and Michael Jackson. Warchild was established in 1994 to benefit Bosnian children, and each year attempts to aid the youth of the world whose countries are troubled by war. This year's show, scheduled for June 1 in Modena, Italy, will raise funds for Kosovo refugees and Guatemalan children. Ricky also performed at the May 16, 1999, Billboard International Latin Music Awards hosted by Daisy Fuentes and Paul Rodriguez. Award presenters include Gloria Estefan, Jon Secada, Carmen Electra, Tito Puente, and Celia Cruz.

Ricky's performance on *Saturday Night Live* on March 8 was just as inspired as ever. His loose trousers and form-fitting shirt accentuated his perpetual-motion hips, and the frenetic energy of the "Livin' La Vida Loca" music video was recreated in the stage set complete with sexy dancers and a pumping brass section.

Everything went completely loco on March 11, when Ricky's English-language debut, simply entitled *Ricky Martin*, hit with a resounding boom. The album entered the *Billboard* charts at Number One, and sold a staggering 661,000 copies in its first week of release—the top weekly sales record for the year. He celebrated the release of the album not by partying into the wee hours and hamming it up with newfound celebrity pals, but with his fans. Skipping from New York to L.A., from Chicago to Miami, he visited record stores to sign copies of the album and chat with his supporters. "I need to have immediate contact with the audience," he explained to Rosie O'Donnell. "I need to know what they think about the album . . . if they like it, I sign the autograph—if they don't like the album, we'll talk business!" It seems he needn't have worried . . . they like it, all right. In-store appearances were truly insane, with thousands and thousands of fans bombarding their favorite new star. Ricky had to be airlifted out of Hollywood by a helicopter due to the Beatles-style chaos his Sunset Strip Tower Records appearance caused. His triumphant appearance at New York City's Tower Records made headlines, with an unprecedented surge of fans bringing gridlock to the streets of Manhattan and causing the NYPD to close down a number of city blocks.

The enthusiasm was palpable, even from record company big wigs who've seen them come and go. "I haven't seen pandemonium like this since early Springsteen," Columbia Records president Don Ienner told *Entertainment Weekly* in its April 23, 1999, issue. "This is a major cultural movement." "Ricky's absolutely electrifying," Sony Music CEO Tommy Mottola raved to *People* magazine in its 1999 "Fifty Most Beautiful"

issue. "He's got this special charisma that comes along only once in a while."

That special charisma was not, it turned out, limited to the high kicks and swivel hips of his onstage persona. Ricky Martin was just as enticing and captivating off-stage. He began appearing on every television show in town, granting interviews from MTV to the morning news. His conversations were punctuated with wide grins and laughs of delight—head thrown back, arms stretched wide. A very physical person, Ricky is full of gestures and eye-twinkling contact. To put it bluntly, he's loving every minute of it, and the feeling is mutual.

Ricky's appearance on the Rosie O'Donnell show the very day of the U.S. release of *Ricky Martin* endeared him even further to American audiences. The candlelit nightclub atmosphere of his performance of "Livin' La Vida Loca" was as joyous as ever; as always, he pulled out all the stops and brought a full cast and crew including silver lamé clad dancing girls and a cool-as-cats brass section. It was his interview with Rosie, however, that really thrilled the audience. His obvious excitement and pride at his burgeoning U.S. success was tempered by his humble and gracious attitude. When Rosie said, "Let me tell you something, America is in love with you!" his unabashed delight at hearing this was as cute as a little boy who's just been told he can have an ice cream. At one point Rosie stopped their conversation to lean over and wipe his sweaty brow (this was just after his usually, shall we say, energetic rendition of his hit single) with her sleeve, joking "I'll never, ever wash this again!" Ricky pulled out a handkerchief he was holding just for that purpose that he had completely forgotten to use—he was far too busy enjoying himself to worry about how he looked. Ricky proceeded to serenade Rosie with a selection from *Les Mis*, and then got her on her feet to teach her a few dance moves. What came across most in this television appearance was Ricky Martin's lack of vanity—coupled with his talent and dedication, it makes for a very appealing package.

"When they say sex symbol, I get a little anxious," Ricky admitted to Gloria Estefan in the June 1999 issue of *Interview*. "Sexuality and sensuality are very different. Sensuality is something you're born with. . . . Unfortunately with the sexual thing in this business, it takes away credibility for some reason, Gloria. I'm not going to think about it. I'm just going to do my music." He went on to explain, "I don't think, Do I have to be sexy or not? I have fun, crack up, have a really good time, shake my body, that's it." But despite his (inexplicable) dismissal of the value of his own good old fashioned sex appeal, he exudes it nonetheless. He did confess to *USA Today* in its May 7, 1999, edition, "I used to freak out every time people would mention the words 'sex symbol.' But I was talking to Gloria Estefan recently, and she said, 'You know what, buddy? If you have it, take advantage of it, 'cause it's not gonna be there forever!' Because we Latins, we are warm-blooded—we meet somebody and we kiss immediately. So Gloria basically said, 'Look, it's part of you—don't be ashamed of it.'"

Ricky Martin, with a top-notch production crew featuring Ricky's now-signature team of Robi Rosa, K.C. Porter, and Desmond Child, as well as Jon Secada, Emilio Estefan, Jr., and even Madonna and William Orbit, is a beautifully crafted piece of work. On this record, the authentic sound of Ricky Martin has really been captured. "Technology is great and it works so you use it, but I also try to keep things very simple," Ricky explained in his IMusic Contemporary Showcase online artist biography. "I don't want my voice to sound too technical, I want it to sound like me. The way I feel is, I don't have to sound perfect, but my emotion has to nail it. There's nothing scientific about it; it's all about emotion. I let it flow. If it's real, it stays."

Even before the C2 Records (a division of Sony Music's Columbia label) release, critics were champing at the bit. "It doesn't take a genius to predict huge success for the first English-language album from this former Menudo singer in light of his spectacular Grammy performance, his chiseled looks, and a hit, 'Livin' la Vida Loca,' that makes everyone in the vicinity feel as if they have a fire in their pants," reasoned New York *Times* columnist Neil Strauss in the paper's April 28, 1999, issue.

Of course, nobody likes a winner, and, as they say, if you can't create, critique. Ernesto Lechner's review in the Los Angeles *Times* May 9, 1999, edition gave *Ricky Martin* only two and a half stars, labeling it a "noisy, sparkling pop extravaganza" with "success written all over it." As so often is the case, critics seem unable to reconcile the concept of success with the concept of talent, decrying any artist who achieves or strives for the former as a traitor to the latter. "Ultimately, Martin's desire to conquer the Anglo market might have been the wrong artistic choice," Lechner writes. "From a one-of-a-kind Latin singer with exquisite taste, he has turned into yet another mainstream pop idol." *Time* magazine, in its May 10, 1999, issue, reasoned, "Ricky is not a great CD, but it is energetic, forceful, and eager to please . . . . This is an unabashed pop record, but it's saved by its Latin soul." Why an artist presenting his fifth solo album to the world cannot be both a mainstream star and a one-of-a-kind singer is a question worth answering. Isn't it a healthy sign that in the domain of Celine Dion there is space for something different? Ricky Martin's aim is not to homogenize himself right out of existence by morphing into a middle of the road American pop star, but to expand the boundaries a little in order to allow his own musical sound to evolve mainstream USA's taste in popular music.

On recording an English-language CD, Ricky is quoted in his IMusic Contemporary Showcase online artist biography as saying, "It's all about communicating. I will never stop singing in Spanish—that's who I am—but this was always part of the plan. . . . I was not going to release this album until I was completely content with what I'd be presenting." The album was actually in the works for two full years, proving that Ricky hasn't rushed to make his big break in the States, but rather has been carefully crafting his English debut in order to ensure that it would stand the test of time. A stop-off at one-hit-wonderland is not on this artist's itinerary. As a show-business veteran, Ricky is well aware of the mechanisms behind fame. He knows how to obtain it, and how difficult it is to maintain it. As he told *Time* magazine in its May 10, 1999, issue, "I want to do this forever. I want to be respected in the States in twenty years. So the first impression is very important." He remains almost stubbornly optimistic, however, refusing to let any doubts plunge him into undue worry; as he told *Entertainment Weekly* in its April 23, 1999, issue, "With all humbleness, I think we'll sell ten million copies." This is, after all,

his dream. "I want to do this forever," he told *USA Today* in its March 1, 1999, edition. "I don't want to be the hit of the summer, and, hopefully, with a lot of humility, we can talk in ten years and I'll still be here."

Each of the fourteen tracks on *Ricky Martin* has something unique to offer. After "Livin' La Vida Loca"'s promise of "new sensations" and "new addictions," that's exactly what we were hoping for. "The link between each song is the Latin taste, is the Latin sound, is the percussion, is the horns, is the passion," Ricky told *MTV News 1515*. And passion is one thing this album has in abundance, be it the slow, smoldering kind or the take-your-clothes-off-and-go-dancing-in-the-rain variety. English-speaking fans will delight in the opportunity to revel in the romantic story-telling quality of songs like "Spanish Eyes" (*I met a girl at the Carnival/In Rio de Janiero*). The album offers up several beautiful ballads—two, "You Stay With Me" and "I Count the Minutes" courtesy of writer Diane Warren (who brought us Leann Rhimes's hit "How Do I Live"). For new Ricky Martin converts who can't get enough of the *vida loca*, there are more beat-crazy tunes to dance to here as well, in particular the infectious "Shake Your Bon-Bon" which makes the most of Latin funk and rock and is chock-full of horns and hot female back-up vocals. Many, many Latin sounds are here for Middle America to sample—and that's not all.

"She's All I Ever Had" is sitar-rich; Ricky's time in India exposed him to new musical sounds and textures. He also claims to have learned a lot about humility and appreciating what one has during his travels there, and cites *The Seven Spiritual Laws of Success* by Deepak Chopra as a valuable life guide. "I Am Made of You" (*I am made of you/You are made of me/And everything you are/Is what I'm meant to be*) is a very spiritual song. Ricky, who was raised a Catholic, is very serious in his exploration of different beliefs. He has studied many religions, including Buddhism, Hinduism, Judaism, and Scientology. "Something that really gives me a lot of comfort is that they are all in search of something. That something is God. And that God is light, serenity, peace, and acceptance," he told *Interview* in its June 1999 issue. On the list of thank-yous on the album's liner notes are the Himalayas, Swami Yogananda Giri, and "God and Guru for guiding me into stillness." That Ricky Martin has been privately and quietly delving into diverse spiritual doctrines without bringing it up in interviews as a vehicle to make himself somehow more interesting is commendable, and goes hand-in-hand with his insistence on keeping private and public lives as separate as possible.

Ricky Martin, the album, features two duets; on "Private Emotion" Ricky sings with Swedish recording artist Meja. It is "Be Careful (Cuidado Con Mi Corazón)" however, his

collaboration with Madonna, that has whipped up the most anticipation. The song, co-written and produced by Madonna and William Orbit, is an airy, entrancing track that seamlessly blends Ricky's Latin sound with Ms. Ciccione's current genre du jour to create an intriguing sort of electronica-ballad. Orbit, best-known Stateside for his work on Madonna's *Ray of Light*, has ensured that this song far exceeds expectations of a chart-pleasing duet between the Queen and upcoming Prince of popular music, and wisely chooses instead to present an original fusion of two talented artists' unique musical visions. "We're thinking about making it the second single," Ricky told MTV News on April 22, 1999. "So we're about to record the video any time soon. It's just a beautiful song." A pinch of drama never did anyone any harm, and an alleged rift between Madonna and Sony CEO (and Mariah Carey's ex-husband) Tommy Mottola spiced up the recording of the duet. It was reported that Mottola attempted to rush the sessions along a bit, which wasn't to the former material girl's liking, but Ricky's charms soon smoothed things over. Whether or not the rumor holds any truth, Ricky was absolutely thrilled at the opportunity to work with Madonna. He told Katie Couric during his March 12, 1999, appearance on the *Today Show* that the experience was "amazing. First of all, she's a living legend—we all know that. Second, she's so talented." He went on to say, "I think it's one of my favorite songs on the album, to be quite honest."

Here's hoping that Ricky Martin will ride this latest wave of success with the wonderful combination of circumspection and all-out appreciation that has stood him in such good stead throughout his career. He is promising his new country full of fans in the United States a North American tour in the fall, with two and a half month's worth of Martinizing beginning in September 1999. He has also reportedly been receiving film scripts by the dozen, and often speaks a little wistfully of returning to the stage, or even writing and producing his own play. It's rumored that he recently turned down an offer to star alongside Jennifer Lopez in a new film version of *West Side Story*, but he hasn't closed the door entirely on his acting career. However, music remains at the top of his list for now. "Music is my priority. A lot of things are going on, and—I want to be humble about it, but I'm very optimistic. I'm very psyched. It's really, really beautiful," he told *USA Today* in its May 7, 1999, edition, adding, "It's a big responsibility. I can open the door to a new generation of Latin performers."

Putting the music, dedication, and, well, sex appeal of Ricky Martin aside for a moment, even the cold hard facts spell long-term Stateside success for Ricky and his fellow Latin music-makers. Latinos are the fastest-growing segment of America's population, slated to knock African Americans off the top of the country's ethnic minority charts by the year 2005. In short, the Latin music business is hot. And it is destined to become white-hot. Of course, all of this hoopla has been brewing and bubbling away for a long, long, time. Let us not forget the heydays of Tito Puente and Desi Arnaz, the nationwide fervor over Ritchie Valens and "La Bamba," the American housewives' adoration of Julio Eglesias, the late Tejano star Selena . . . the list goes on and on. It is surely much to the satisfaction of hard-working, seasoned promoters of Latin music like Gloria and producer-husband Emilio Estefan that the beats, rhythms, and sounds they broke out of Miami into middle America are now being welcomed with open arms. As Emilio told *Time* magazine in its May 24, 1999, issue, "None of this could have happened fifteen years ago. Gloria and I went through the hardest part. A dozen years ago, a label threw me out when I tried to use congas on a recording . . . . The younger generation is now reacting to Latin music." Before Ricky had even completed his pre-album-release press campaign, names of other crossover breakthroughs were being bandied about.

Sure-fire candidates for the next wave in U.S. popular music are salsa star Marc Anthony; Shakira, Columbia's top female rocker; Spain's son of Julio, Enrique Iglesias; Puerto Rican merengue king Elvis Crespo; Latin heartthrob Carlos Ponce, also hailing from Puerto Rico; and Mexican classic rock group Mana. Screen star Jennifer Lopez—who played Selena in the movie tribute to the life of the ill-fated star—has her own debut album entitled *On the Six* poised to top the charts. Top gun Tommy Mottola told *Time* magazine in its May 15, 1999, issue, "I have no crystal ball, but my gut tells me that Latin music can be the next big reservoir of talent for mainstream superstars."

Ricky remains, throughout all the fervor and the newfound American fascination with the "Latin Lover" who has burst on the scene, consistently quiet on the subject of his private life. It is the one thing he is not prepared to sacrifice for his career. To queries about the nature of his relationship with television presenter Rebecca de Alba, he says only that she is working in Spain these days. He resorts to generalizations when asked about the opposite sex, and described his ideal mate to *Rolling Stone* in its April 29, 1999, issue, stating, "I need someone who's not afraid to suck, someone risky, someone who's not in a pose all the time. But I also need a woman who behaves like a woman, who knows how to sit at the table and all that." As he told MTV's Serena Altschul, "I sell tickets to my concerts, I sell CDs, but the day I feel forced to sell the key to my room, I'll stop doing this."

Ricky hasn't forgotten his roots. He is the spokesperson for Puerto Rican tourism, the face and voice behind the logo "Puerto Rico Sounds Better Than Ever." The TV ad campaign, featuring Ricky smoothly dancing in front of a back-drop of colorful scenes and saying, "Only Puerto Rico sounds like this" is supremely effective; it makes your average viewer want to jump up and pack their bags. "It's all about breaking stereotypes," Ricky insisted to *Entertainment Weekly* in its April 23, 1999, issue. "For me, the fact that people think Puerto Rico is *Scarface*, that we ride donkeys to school—that has to change."

Nowadays when Ricky returns to Puerto Rico, he is greeted with even more feverish devotion. Could it be that the people of his homeland are relieved that he hasn't forgotten them in the clamor and excitement of his burgeoning American recognition? On one recent occasion tens of thousands of adoring fans congested the environs of San Juan's Aeropuerto Internacional when their beloved Ricky flew into the capital city, forcing him to forego the five-minute car journey to his first stop—a press conference, of course—in favor of a helicopter lift. Home away from home for Ricky, when he's not on the road, may be his house on the bay in Miami. But his family, friends, and fans in Puerto Rico needn't worry—the first thing Ricky Martin always does once he finds his seat on an airplane is to look at a map to get his bearings and see how far he is from home.

DISCOGRAPHY

ALBUMS:

RICKY MARTIN
Fuego Contra Fuego / Dime Que Me Quieres (Bring a Little Lovin) / Vuelo / Conmigo Nadie Puede (Comigo Ninguem Pode) / Te Voy a Conquistar (Vou te Conquistar) / Juego de Ajedrez / Corazon entre Nubes (Coracao Nas Nuvens) / Ser Feliz / El Amor de Mi Vida / Susana / Popotitos
1991 Sony Discos CD-80695

ME AMARAS
No Me Pidas Mas / Es Mejor Decirse Adios / Entre el Amor Y Los Halagos / Lo Que Nos Pase, Pasara / Ella Es / Me Amaras / Ayudame / Eres Como el Aire / Que Dia es Hoy (Self Control) / Hooray! Hooray! (It's a Holi-Holiday)
1993 Sony Discos CDZ-81044/2-470746

A MEDIO VIVIR
Fuego de Noche, Nieve de Dia / A Medio Vivir / Maria / Te Extraño, Te Olvido, Te Amo / Donde Estaras / Volveras / Revolucion / Somos la Semilla / Como Decirte Adios / Bombom de Azucar / Corazon / Nada es Imposible
1995 Sony Discos CDZ-81651/2-479882

VUELVE
Por Arriba, Por Abajo / Vuelve / Lola, Lola / Casi un Bolero / Corazonado / La Bomba / Hagamos El Amor / La Copa de la Vida (Spanish) / Perdido Sin Ti / Asi Es La Vida / Marcia Baila / No Importa La Distancia / Gracias Por Pensar en Mi / Casi un Bolero (Instrumental)
1998 Sony Discos CDF-82653/2-488789

RICKY MARTIN
Livin' La Vida Loca / Spanish Eyes / She's All I Ever Had / Shake Your Bon-Bon / Be Careful (Cuidado Con Mi Corazó) / I Am Made Of You / Love You For A Day / Private Emotion / The Cup of Life (Spanglish Radio Edit) / You Stay With Me / Livin' La Vida Loca (Spanish Version) / I Count The Minutes / Bella (She's All I Ever Had) / Maria (Spanglish Radio Edit)
1999 C2 Records (Columbia) CK69891

SINGLES:

MARIA
Maria (Spanglish Radio Edit) / Maria (Spanish Radio Edit) / Maria (Spanglish Extended) / Maria (Spanish Extended) / Maria (Spanglish Dub) / Maria (Perc A Pella Mix)
1996 Sony/Columbia 78351

UN DOS TRES MARIA
1997 Sony 4765

THE CUP OF LIFE
English Radio Edit / Spanish Radio Edit / Spanglish Radio Edit / Dub of Life Mix / Spanglish Radio Edit / Jason Nevin's Remix
1998 Sony

THE CUP OF LIFE
The Cup of Life / Maria
1998 Sony 78932

LA BOMBA (THE REMIXES)
La Bomba (Spanglish) / La Bomba (Radio Remix) / La Bomba (Dub Mix) / La Bomba (Long Version Remix) / La Bomba 1998 Sony Discos

LA BOMBA, PT. 2
La Bomba (Spanglish Version) / La Bomba (Remix-Radio Edit) / La Bomba (Remix-Long Version) / La Bomba (Remix – Dub Mix) 1999 Sony 66348B

LIVIN' LA VIDA LOCA (THE REMIXES)
Livin' La Vida Loca (English version) / Livin' La Vida Loca (Spanish version) April 1999

LIVIN' LA VIDA LOCA
Album Version / Scissorhands / Push & Pull English House Mix / Track Masters Remix / Pablo Flores English Radio Edit / Pablo Flores Spanish Dub-apella
1999 C2 Records (Columbia) 44K79153

COMPILATIONS:

BOLEROS VOZ Y SENTIMIENTO, VOL. 1
features Corazon – Ricky Martin
1993 Sony Discos 80954

EXITOS 93
features Fuego Contra Fuego– Ricky Martin
1993 Globo Records 80970

HEY JUDE . . . TRIBUTO A LOS BEATLES
features Day Tripper – Ricky Martin
1995 Globo Records 81526

VOCES UNIDAS
1996 Capital/EMI Latin Records 36283

NAVIDAD EN LAS AMERICAS
features What Child is This – Ricky Martin
Disney Records 67626-2

MUSIC OF THE WORLD CUP: ALLEZ! OLA! OLE!
features The Cup Of Life (Official Song Of The World Cup) - Ricky Martin
1998 T-Neck Records 69344